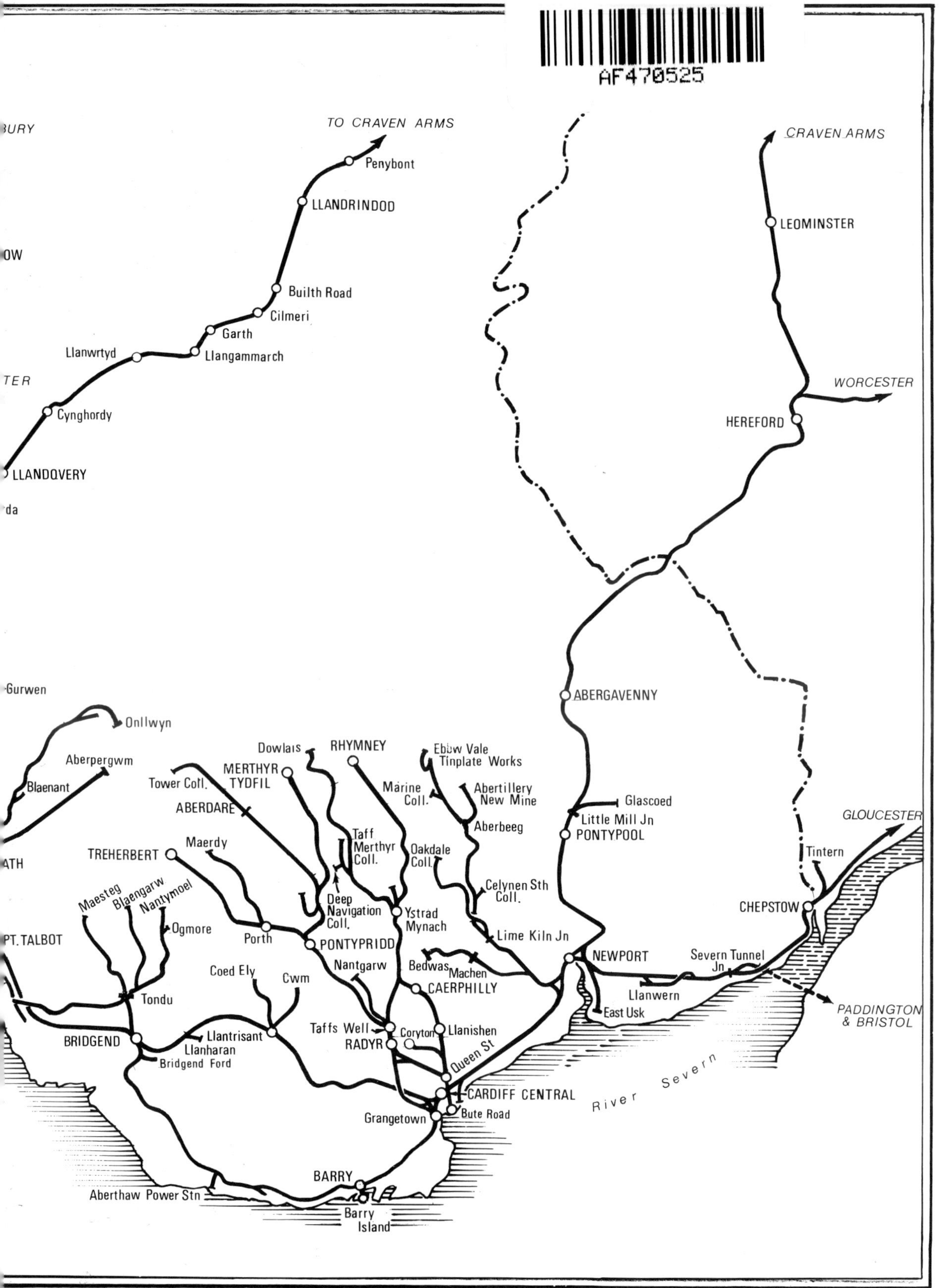
TO CRAVEN ARMS
Penybont
LLANDRINDOD
Builth Road
Cilmeri
Garth
Llanwrtyd
Llangammarch
Cynghordy
LLANDOVERY
CRAVEN ARMS
LEOMINSTER
WORCESTER
HEREFORD
Gurwen
Onllwyn
Aberpergwm
Blaenant
Tower Coll.
MERTHYR TYDFIL
ABERDARE
Dowlais
RHYMNEY
Ebbw Vale Tinplate Works
Marine Coll.
Abertillery New Mine
Aberbeeg
ABERGAVENNY
Glascoed
Little Mill Jn
PONTYPOOL
GLOUCESTER
Tintern
TREHERBERT
Maerdy
Taff Merthyr Coll.
Oakdale Coll.
Celynen Sth Coll.
Deep Navigation Coll.
Ystrad Mynach
Lime Kiln Jn
Maesteg
Blaengarw
Nantymoel
Ogmore
PT. TALBOT
Porth
PONTYPRIDD
CHEPSTOW
NEWPORT
Severn Tunnel Jn
Bedwas
Machen
Nantgarw
CAERPHILLY
Coed Ely
Cwm
Tondu
Llanwern
East Usk
PADDINGTON & BRISTOL
BRIDGEND
Llantrisant
Llanharan
Bridgend Ford
Taffs Well
RADYR
Coryton
Llanishen
Queen St
CARDIFF CENTRAL
River Severn
Bute Road
Grangetown
BARRY
Aberthaw Power Stn
Barry Island

WESTERN REGION IN WALES

Right: Class 37 No 37.235 seen near St Fagans in August 1980.

WESTERN REGION IN WALES

James McGregor

LONDON

IAN ALLAN LTD

To Victoria Jayne and Stephanie Jayne

All photographs by the Author unless otherwise credited

Front cover: Nos 37.297 and 37.282 pass Baglan, between Briton Ferry and Port Talbot, on the South Wales main line with a loaded mgr train en route for Aberthaw on 25 March 1982.

Back cover, top: No 253.013, right, waits to depart from Swansea High Street station with the 07.10 service to Paddington on 4 January 1982. No 37.178 stands at the head of the empty stock on the left.

Back cover, bottom: Who said Class 03 locomotives are not amphibious? Nos 03.119, 03.142 and 03.120 seem set to take the plunge as they lead a train of coal from Coedbach washery on the Cwmmawr line. This photograph superbly illustrates one of the problems experienced by British Rail in operating the Burry Port & Gwendraeth Valley line, where flooding frequently plays havoc at the Burry Port end of the track. The other problem of low clearances necessitates the use of Class 03 traction. The building of a new link from the Gwendraeth Valley branch to Kidwelly is expected to cure these problems in 1984. *Bob Masterman*

Previous page: Nos 56.044 and 56.040 *Oystermouth* approach Cardiff with their train of empty iron ore wagons from Llanwern to Port Talbot on the morning of 14 April 1982. *Bob Masterman*

Far right: The 10.46 Shrewsbury-Swansea arrives at Llandeilo more than half an hour late on 30 June 1981. With the number of loco-hauled trains on the Central Wales line being kept to a minimum, the track testing vehicle had been attached to the rear of this train, which affected the progress of this 2-car DMU set. The track testing car seen here is an ex-GWR vehicle.

First published 1983

ISBN 0 7110 1276 8

Published by Ian Allan Ltd, Shepperton, Surrey; and printed by Ian Allan Printing Ltd at their works at Coombelands in Runnymede, England

Contents

C603

Introduction

The philosophy behind the compilation of this album has been one of attempting to portray a view of the modern railway scene in South Wales during the early 1980s. I have defined my geographical area of interest as the part of the railway network which falls within the National boundary of Wales and which is operated by the Western Region of British Rail. Within this context I have aimed to create as balanced a view as possible of the types of train, the variety of traction and the variety of scenery encountered in the area.

The recession has accelerated the already steady industrial and economic decline of South Wales, but in spite of the obvious implications for British Rail, the area has managed to maintain its position as one of the most interesting and vital parts of the national rail network. In terms of published railway photography however, South Wales must sadly be regarded as rather a neglected part of the world. My hope therefore is that this book might to some extent help stimulate a greater interest in the area.

During the early 1980s changes have taken place in British Rail's passenger and freight operations both nationwide and within South Wales. The introduction of HSTs on cross-country passenger services has marked a further decline in the number of locomotive-hauled passenger trains. Possibly one of the most striking changes though, has been the introduction of Class 33 traction on to many services in the area. Once considered to be a rare visitor to Wales, Class 33 traction is now well established on Cardiff to Crewe services and on many of the passenger services, to and from the South of England. More recently Class 33s have found themselves on services to West Wales. Regarding freight operations the early 1980s have seen the final demise of British Rail's collect and deliver service. It is planned that by 1984 the more traditional wagon-load freights will be totally phased out, as more concentrated effort is put into the development of Freightliner and Speedlink services.

While making this album I have travelled several thousands of miles within South Wales and have, almost without exception, been impressed by the friendliness of the many railwaymen I have met. Most seemed to be genuinely interested in my project and all were very generous with their words of advice, which has been most warmly appreciated. It would be impossible to mention by name all the people who have helped, though the contribution of certain individuals is worthy of special mention. Thanks are due to Keith Hayward and Bob Masterman for their encouragement and for providing me with transport at times when I preferred not to venture out on my motorcycle; to Alan Langley for his help with the laborious task of typing the manuscript. The help given to me by Neil Sprinks has been invaluable, and many has been the occasion that I have needed to call upon his comprehensive knowledge of the railways in South Wales. I should especially like to thank my wife June, without whose sympathy and patience this book would not have been possible.

James McGregor
Cardiff
July 1982

Below: No 47.501 crosses the old bascule-bridge over the River Tywi at Carmarthen as it departs with the 11.25 ecs to Fishguard Harbour on 30 December 1981. The train had formed the 10.20 Swansea-Carmarthen and was going on to form the 13.15 Fishguard Harbour-Paddington service.

West Wales Passenger Services

Left: Locomotives without any form of train heating are often seen at the head of summer passenger services. Here one such locomotive, No 47.351, blasts out of Spittal tunnel with the 13.15 Fishguard Harbour-Paddington train on 5 September 1981. Spittal tunnel is between Letterston Junction and Clarbeston Road and the width of the tunnel and adjacent formation reveals that this section of the Fishguard line was formerly double track.

Below: British Rail engineers make repairs to a farm bridge at Barre farm to the east of Narberth on the Pembroke Dock-Whitland line as a Class 47 locomotive leads the 08.50 (SO) service from Pembroke Dock to Paddington on 5 September 1981. The telephoto lens employed in this photograph emphasises the change in the gradient of the track at this point.

Above: The final section, from Johnston, of the line to Milford Haven is single track. Here the driver of No 37.179 with the 11.15 Swansea-Milford Haven train is seen accepting the token from the signalman at Johnston signalbox on 3 September 1981.

Right: The 13.15 Fishguard Harbour-Swansea train, which is led by No 37.192, passes farm buildings at Hendre-fach on the Fishguard Harbour branch on 3 September 1981.

Above: Travelling at high speed No 47.500 *Great Western* leads the 09.27 Paddington-Fishguard Harbour train through the beautifully wooded Treffgarne Gorge between Clarbeston Road and Letterston Junction on 4 September 1981.

Left: Failed DMU No C615 is towed into Clarbeston Road by No 37.190 en route for Milford Haven with the 13.15 service from Swansea on 3 September 1981. Failure at Gowerton meant that the train was running 90 minutes late. Note that the locomotive is fitted with miniature snow ploughs, perhaps in early anticipation of the severe weather conditions of January 1982?

Left: An intersting service which was dropped from the 1982-3 passenger timetable was the 07.45 Tuesdays, Thursdays and Saturdays-only Pembroke Dock to Port Talbot. This service enabled ferry passengers from Ireland to link up at Port Talbot with the Paddington-bound HST services. The train is seen on 31 December 1981 on the Swansea District line at Grovesend on a route primarily used by freight.

Below left: No 37.189 with the 16.10 Swansea-Pembroke Dock is seen on the 5 September 1981 on its approach to Kidwelly station.

Right: The same loco No 37.189 is seen the day before, heading a train of empty stock to Fishguard Harbour. The train had previously formed the 10.20 Swansea-Carmarthen and was going forward to form the 13.15 Fishguard Harbour-Paddington. Here the train is seen passing through a deep cutting on its approach to Spittal tunnel.

Below: No 37.236 reaches the end of the line as it arrives at Pembroke Dock with the 16.10 train from Swansea on 3 September 1981. The station was extensively renovated in 1980 following the transfer of the B&I line's ferry operations from the port of Swansea to Pembroke Dock.

Above: The 13.15 Fishguard Harbour-Paddington train passes the village of St Georges on its approach to Cardiff on 13 June 1981.

Centre left: The introduction of summer timetables produce some interesting through train services. One such service is the 08.24 (SO) York-Tenby service which is seen running on the main line near St Fagans west of Cardiff on 20 June 1981 with No 47.109 at the head.

Below left: Unit No C621 which is fitted with a headlight for operation on the Central Wales line, is seen standing at the Milford Haven terminus waiting to depart with the 17.25 service to Swansea on 3 September 1981.

Top right: An unusual view of Swansea High Street station from the adjacent High Street carriage sidings, shows No 47.420 departing more than an hour late with the 12.05 train to Fishguard Harbour on 31 December 1981. Delays to incoming connecting services, due to flooding, had prompted the late departure of this train.

Right: Manorbier station on the Pembroke Dock-Whitland line is the only place in South Wales where regular passenger trains must wait whilst the train's guard opens the gates of an unmanned crossing. No 37.236 waits patiently at the head of the 18.35 Pembroke Dock to Swansea train as the guard performs his duties on a bright evening in September 1981.

Top right: The power provided by Nos 33.025 *Sultan* and 33.018 seems excessive for the four-carriage 17.20 Swansea-Cardiff which was seen on 7 June 1982 passing through the countryside near Llantrisant. Class 33 traction was introduced on services to West Wales at the same time as the 1982-3 timetable.

Right: Until the introduction of the 1982-3 timetable this Class 101 Metro-Cammell DMU was often seen on services between Cardiff and Severnside and was numbered B813. Now with the B prefix erased DMU set No 813 has been transferred to run on services west of Swansea. Here the three-car set is seen arriving at Pembrey & Burry Port station with the 16.15 Pembroke Dock-Swansea on 29 May 1982.

Below: The 13.40 Milford Haven-Swansea train departs from the terminus on 28 May 1981. No 37.180 *Sir Dyfed/County of Dyfed* is in ex-works condition following its official naming earlier on in the day at Carmarthen, from where the locomotive worked the 11.15 Swansea-Milford Haven service. Note the Milford Haven sleeper on its daily sojourn in the carriage siding.

Merry-go-round trains

Above: Merry-go-round trains are frequently seen in South Wales and the majority have Aberthaw Power Station as their destination. This photograph however, shows a Llanharan to Didcot mgr train headed by No 47.234 and a Class 56 locomotive passing Roath Coal Sidings on 10 July 1981. Combined, these locomotives produce almost 6,000hp for the climb out of the Severn Tunnel to Patchway.

Left: It is difficult to imagine that this attractive rural setting falls within the city boundary of Cardiff. A pair of Class 37s led by No 37.282 head the Aberthaw-bound train over the Radyr-Penarth curve line, on a hot summer's day in July 1981. *Keith Hayward*

Above: Aberthaw Power Station's insatiable appetite for coal requires that several mgrs are diagrammed to run at weekends. Empties in the charge of No 37.294 and 37.287 are bound for Cwmbargoed and are seen shortly after branching off the Rhymney Valley line south of Ystrad Mynach station on a Saturday working on 4 July 1981.

Right: The double-tracked line between Walnut Tree and Aber Junctions is known to local railwaymen as 'the big hill'. The exhaust fumes exuding from Nos 37.270 and 37.286 with a train of empties bear witness to the steep gradient. The vertical columns visible in the photograph are the remains of the old Barry Railway.

Above: A trackside view of the 'big hill' shows Nos 37.247 and 37.293 leading a train of empty mgr wagons towards Aber Junction and the Rhymney Valley line, on 4 September 1981. *Bob Masterman*

Left: Having worked through the loop at the power station and had the train's load of 1,100 tonnes of coal discharged, No 47.182 returns the empties to sidings on the main line at Aberthaw on 4 March 1981. Although double-headed Class 37s are responsible for bringing coal from the collieries, the last short stage of the journey from Aberthaw to the power station is the responsibility of Class 47 locos fitted with the special slow speed control. This control is brought into use when the trains are unloaded while moving at a constant speed of 0.5mph. The exaggerated perspective of the telephoto lens shows clearly the results to the track of the continuous pounding from up to 20 mgr trains a day. The track was renewed in July 1981.

Below: Nos 37.287 and 37.294 with a train load of coal from Cwmbargoed join the branch from Taff Merthyr and Deep Navigation collieries at the site of the former Nelson & Llancaiach station on 4 July 1981. Engineering work during March 1982 saw the removal of this junction and its repositioning at the farther end of the former station.

Bottom: Nos 37.270 and 37.286 wait patiently as their train is loaded at Penallta Colliery on 29 July 1981. The branch to Penallta departs from the Rhymney Valley line just to the north of Ystrad Mynach station.

Top: Mechanical shovels load a mgr train at Deep Navigation Colliery, Treharris on 8 September 1981. Nos 37.244 and 37.278 edge the train forward during the loading procedure before conveying their traffic to Aberthaw.

Above: Newport Transporter Bridge provides a suitable backdrop for this study of No 56.046 as it leads a train of empty mgr wagons from Didcot into the Newport Dock complex on 30 September 1980. Such trains came to an end when the Central Electricity Generating Board ceased coal imports through Newport.
John Chalcraft

Top: Nos 37.205 and 37.257 are ready to depart for Aberthaw following the loading of their train with opencast coal at Cwmbargoed on 8 September 1981.

Above: A fine view of Aberthaw Power Station and the sea is provided here as No 37.295 and 37.286 lead empties west along the Vale of Glamorgan line on 20 March 1982. *John Chalcraft*

Right: An unusual locomotive to head an internal South Wales mgr is No 56.035 *Taff Merthyr*. The naming of the locomotive in a ceremony at Taff Merthyr Colliery earlier in the day on 9 November 1981, provided the special reason for Class 56 haulage. The train, en route from Taff Merthyr to Aberthaw is approaching Nelson where coal stocks at Deep Navigation Colliery are seen on the left. *Keith Hayward*

Below: Brynlliw Colliery, just south of Pontarddulais is the most westerly South Wales Colliery to provide a mgr service to Aberthaw. Here a mechanical shovel and a crane with grab, load the 05.10 empties-working from Aberthaw on 4 July 1981. No 37.231 and 37.279 are in charge of this train. *Bob Ranson*

Bottom: After the loading of their mgr train at the Neath Abbey Wharf Sidings of Steel Supply Co (Western) Ltd, Nos 37.205 and 37.296 wait to continue their journey to Jersey Marine Junction South, where the locomotives run round before proceding to Aberthaw via Bridgend.

Services to Paddington

Above: The 08.15 Paddington-Swansea train passes over the Neath & Brecon line on 25 March 1982. The Neath & Brecon junction signalbox can be seen to the left of picture and stands at the junction of the former Great Western, Vale of Neath line which now terminates at Aberpergwm and the former Neath & Brecon line which now terminates at Onllwyn. The track between the junction and Jersey Marine has now been singled.

Left: Framed by floral decorations at Cardiff Central station No 253.011 awaits departure from Platform 2 with the 10.10 service to Paddington on 7 August 1981. *Bob Masterman*

Top right: On Sundays engineers often take possession of the Swansea to Cardiff main line, making diversions along the Vale of Glamorgan line relatively common. On 22 February 1981 the diverted 13.20 Swansea-Paddington is seen easing its way at a mere 15mph past the disused, and since demolished signalbox at Aberthaw Cement Works.

Right: A low evening sun provides the backlighting for the 18.15 Paddington-Swansea as it passes East Usk Junction on the approach to Newport on 1 August 1981.

Parcels
Way out
Left luggage
Ladies
Gentlemen
Litter
253 015

Above left: The scenery in South Wales provides some interesting contrasts, here a Paddington-Swansea HST passes the peaceful rural setting near St Georges, west of Cardiff on 20 August 1981.

Left: A Sunday diversion in the form of the 13.15 Paddington-Swansea service is seen passing through Barry station on 15 February 1981, and is about to run on to the Vale of Glamorgan line for Bridgend.

Above: Only one return HST service a day works out of Carmarthen and because of the early morning departure and late evening arrival of the return working, HSTs running west of Swansea can only be photographed during the summer. This photograph shows No 253.024 passing Pembrey & Burry Port station with an empty stock working from Carmarthen to Swansea. Earlier the HST had formed the 16.45 Paddington to Carmarthen. An on track tamping and lining machine rests in the down sidings. *Bob Masterman*

Right: The diverted Sunday 10.15 Paddington-Swansea service formed by No 253.016, is seen crossing Porthkerry Viaduct on the Vale of Glamorgan line immediately west of Barry on 18 September 1981.

Top: The 14.20 Swansea-Paddington service is seen at the point of diversion leaving the main line, which curves to the left of photo and joins the Vale of Glamorgan line just east of Bridgend station on 6 December 1981.

Above: Another diversionary route often employed in South Wales is the one from Bridgend to Port Talbot via Tondu. Here the 08.15 Paddington-Swansea, left, passes the 10.10 up train at the former Tondu station on Sunday 24 May 1982.

Engineering trains

Above: As almost the entire British nation celebrates the Royal Wedding of the Prince of Wales and Lady Diana Spencer the work must still go on. Here ballast is being laid down from Seacow hoppers as part of track renewal operations between Aberthaw Power Station and Aberthaw on 29 July 1981.

Left: In January 1982 South Wales had some of its worst weather in living memory. A two-day continuous snow fall was followed by almost a week of freezing conditions. Practically all tracks in South Wales were rendered impassable at some stage. Here on 15 January engineers are attempting to free frozen points at Cadoxton to allow the snowplough train consisting of Nos 37.305 and 31.209 to clear the track down to Barry docks. The normal passenger timetable was suspended and the Barry-Cardiff Central shuttle service in the guise of Nos C452 and C301 is seen approaching Cadoxton station.

Above: Having managed to negotiate the points at Cadoxton the snowplough train met further problems on its way towards Barry docks. Here, by the ruins of the old Barry Docks signalbox, the leading plough became derailed by thick snow which had been dumped across the tracks following clearance of an adjacent road.

Left: Since a ban was placed on heavy locomotive-haulage on the Central Wales Line in January 1981, few such trains have been noted. From time to time however, exceptions are made; here No 37.291 leads a weedkiller train into Llandovery on 17 May 1982. *Tom Clift*

Top right: The soft early morning winter sunshine illuminates No 37.248 on an engineers train at Abercarn in the Gwent Western Valley on 6 December 1981. The engineers work involved the replacement of points some few hundred metres further along the track.

Right: No 47.338 with a train of ballast and railway sleepers passes Cadoxton on the outskirts of Barry after working on the Vale of Glamorgan line on 2 August 1981. The housing estate on the right stands on the site of former Barry Railway coal stabling sidings and the railway's main route inland to the valleys via Wenvoe.

Left: No 37.189 is seen running on the 'wrong' line during an engineer's possession of the South Wales main line at Pencoed. The train of empties is heading west towards Bridgend on 6 December 1981.

Below: No 47.226 was seen at the head of a train of spoil as it curved towards Barry shortly after working out of the station at Barry Island on 15 February, 1981.

Right: No 25.124 provides the traction for a train of railway sleepers recovered from Cardiff docks on 10 June 1981. The train is seen approaching the South Wales main line near Pengam.

Below right: No 37.278 is in attendance as engineers get on with the job of relaying track just north of Caerphilly tunnel on Sunday 15 February 1981. British Rail made alternative arrangements for passengers wishing to travel to destinations on the Rhymney Valley line. The buildings in the background were originally the GWR Caerphilly locomotive works.

Above: No 37.208 basks in sunshine at the rear of Barry station on 2 August 1981 with a train of recovered ballast.

Left: Travelling near Llandow on the Vale of Glamorgan line on 7 May 1982, is No 47.026 hauling a track testing train. The trailing vehicle of this train is the BR High Speed Track Recording Coach based on a Mk 2F body shell on B5 bogies and capable of running in High Speed Train formations at speeds of up to 125mph.

Bottom left: No 37.233 heads a train of rails and ballast which is being unloaded just to the north of Quaker's Yard station on the Merthyr line on a dull damp day on 6 December 1981.

Right: Major engineering work at Trehafod in the Rhondda Valley was required in the spring of 1982, when a new by-pass resulted in the need to realign the up platform and running line. Here on Sunday 28 March, No 37.279 is seen at the head of a ballast train north of the station. On the left is the disused and bricked up, but modern, Eirw Branch Junction signalbox.

Below: An engineer's ballast train, in the charge of No 37.278, runs 'wrong' line at Peterston on the South Wales main line on 29 March 1980. The cant of the track at this point is as much as 7 degrees.
Bob Ranson

Bottom: It is a rare sight to see the Speno Railgrinder train in action because most of its work is carried out during the hours of darkness. Here the railgrinder is seen running, though not working, on the South Wales main line at Llantrisant on 7 June 1982.

Top: No 37.176, with a weedkiller train, pulls away from the old station at Trethomas and heads back along the Bedwas branch towards Park Junction on 22 May 1982. Bedwas colliery commands the background.

Above: A train load of ballast led by No 37.278 is seen standing south of Abercynon station, where track relaying work was underway on 6 December 1981.

Top: A viaduct inspection unit is manoeuvred into place by No 37.232 on the viaduct over Nant Hir at Seven Sisters on the Onllwyn branch on 11 June 1982.

Above: Nos 03.152 and 03.119 lead a train of empty sleeper wagons towards Sugar Loaf tunnel on the Central Wales line on Sunday 16 May 1982. Sleepers were unloaded during the run between Pantyffynnon and Llanwrtyd. The train is seen here on the return journey south when periodic stops were made to pick up scrap. The headlight which is used on trains operating the Central Wales line can be seen attached to the chimney of the second locomotive, the leading locomotive also had a headlight attached.

Right: A weedkiller train arrives at Tondu signalbox on 18 May 1982 after working on the Ogmore Vale branch. Earlier in the day it had worked on the Tondu-based Maesteg and Blaengarw branches.

CYCLING PROHIBITED

Local services in the valleys and around Cardiff

Below left: DMU No C301, which formed the 17.08 Barry Island to Rhymney service, is seen on the final stage of its journey, as it crosses the viaduct at Pontlottyn on 17 August 1981.

Below: The end of the line at Treherbert as No C331 waits to depart with the 14.35 Sunday service to Barry Island on 28 June 1981. The former line beyond Treherbert passed through the two-mile Rhondda tunnel to the Afan Valley. Passenger services from Treherbert to Bridgend via Cymmer Afan, Maesteg and Tondu ceased in 1970, though from 1968 trouble with subsidence in the Rhondda tunnel had caused the service along the Treherbert to Cymmer Afan section to be replaced by buses.

Above left: It is always encouraging to see a busy and bustling platform. Unit Nos C138 and C450 were coupled together to form the 13.32 Treherbert to Barry Island service, which is seen approaching Ystrad Rhondda station on 12 September 1981. The track nearer the camera is out of use following the singling of this Rhondda Fawr line north of Porth when a new Cardiff Valleys timetable was introduced on 30 March 1981.

Left: The driver returns the token to the signalman at Heath Junction signalbox as the 10.00 Coryton to Cardiff Central train leaves the single track Coryton branch and joins the Rhymney Valley line on 12 September 1981.

Top: A train of two three-car DMUs is surrounded by some typical valleys' scenery shortly after departing from Treherbert on 12 September 1981 with the 12.32 train to Barry Island.

Right: With the withdrawal of passenger services from the Penarth-Cadoxton line in 1968, Penarth became a passenger terminus. Here No C314 waits to depart with the 18.17 Penarth-Rhymney service on 21 July 1981.

Above: The line to the north of Bargoed is singled and before proceeding north drivers collect a token from the signalbox at the end of the station platform. Having received the token the driver of No C335 prepares to depart with the 16.11 Penarth-Rhymney service on 17 August 1981.

Left: The 17.25 Sunday-service from Cardiff Queen Street approaches Dinas Powys en route to Barry Island on 2 August 1981.

Below: A dreary and depressing scene meets the traveller to Cardiff Bute Road where litter and debris abound. Bute Road sees a busy flow of commuters on weekdays but on Saturday 13 June 1981 few passengers joined the 09.35 service to Coryton. The bricked-up building, left, is a one-time Headquarters office of the Taff Vale Railway.

The greenery surrounding Coryton station provides a pleasing contrast to the litter at the Bute Road terminus. The driver of unit No C305 had a few minutes to pause before departing with the 08.02 to Bute Road on 13 June 1981.

Far left: The driver collects the token at Porth station before departing with the 13.00 Barry Island-Treherbert service which was formed by Nos C304 and C306 on 12 September 1981.

Left: In another reminder of the adverse weather conditions in 1982, Derby Class 116 unit No C312 arrives at Aber station in the Rhymney Valley with a southbound service on 12 January. Services ran only when conditions permitted, however, trains did manage to run at a time when the public were being strongly advised to keep their cars off the roads. *Bob Masterman*

Bottom left: The 12.00 Barry Island-Treherbert service formed by Nos C450 and C318, climbs the gradient north of Llwynypia station on 12 September 1981. The former up track had not, at this stage, been lifted.

Right: Bargoed viaduct is traversed by a six-car DMU combination led by No C450 which formed the 17.11 Cardiff-Rhymney service on 17 August 1981.

Below: No C302 enters Llanishen station with an up Rhymney Valley passenger service in July 1981. *Keith Hayward*

Depots and Stabling Points

Left: Despite the recent flurry of naming ceremonies in South Wales, the attaching of locomotive nameplates cannot be regarded by railwaymen as routine work. Here at Canton Depot nameplates were attached to No 56.038 *Western Mail* on 1 June 1981, the day before the official naming ceremony.

Above: Diesel-electric shunter No 08.658 stands alongside diesel mechanical shunter No 03.142 at Landore on 31 December 1981. The Landore based Class 03s have cut down cabs and are used on the Burry Port & Gwendraeth Valley line as well as the Central Wales line freight service from Llanelli to Llandeilo and Llandovery.

Right: Landore Depot had a popular and well attended Open Day on 30 August 1980. A DMU shuttle was operated from Swansea High Street station to convey passengers to the depot. Enthusiasts are seen disembarking from No C602 which had been temporarily relieved of its duties on the Central Wales line.

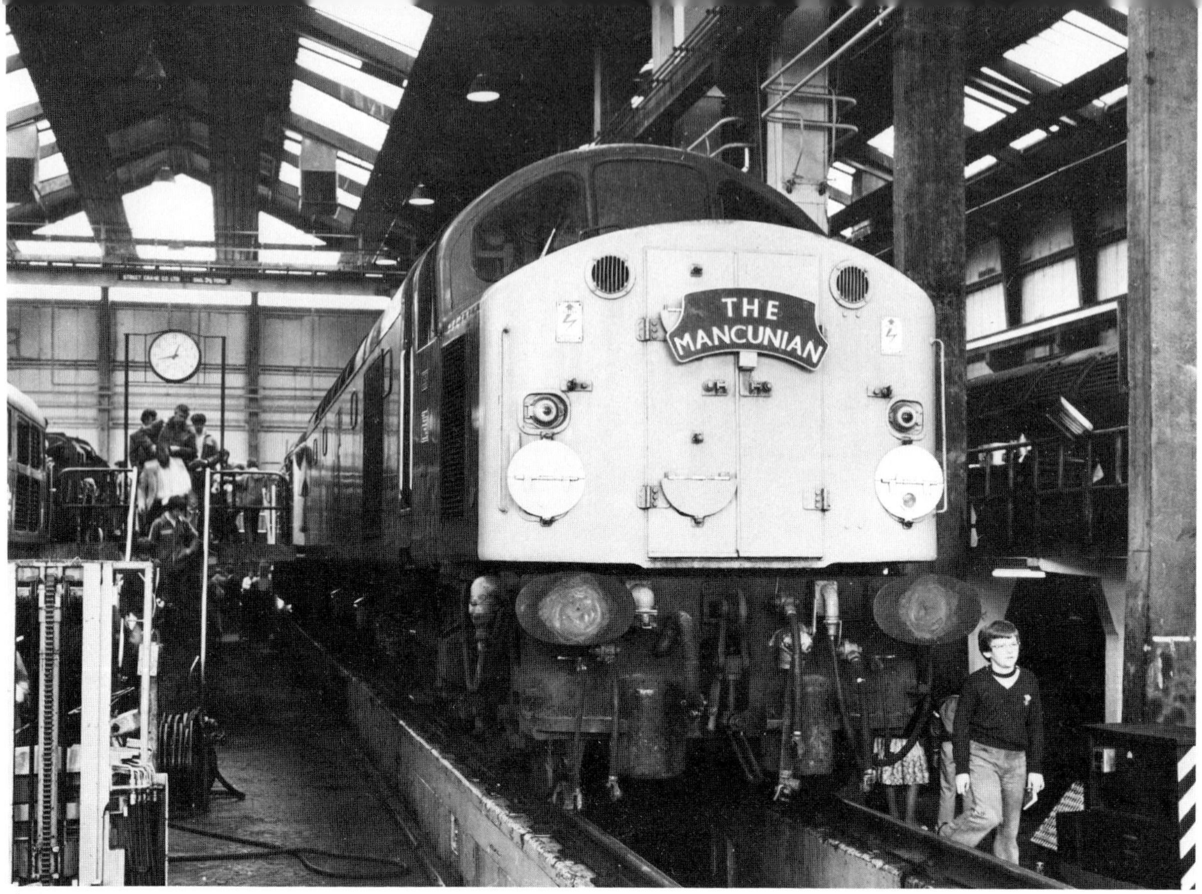

Above left: The appearance of No 40.079 with 'The Mancunian' headboard provided enthusiasts with a chance of taking a closer look at this popular, but locally rare, class of locomotive at Landore Open Day.

Left: Other unusual visitors to South Wales which appeared at the Open Day included No 20.087, 20.042 and 50.047 *Swiftsure*. *British Rail*

Above: The lack of any substantial freight movements at weekends can provide the possibility of seeing a relatively large number of locomotives at depots and stabling points. This photograph shows a variety of locomotives at Severn Tunnel Junction on Saturday 1 August 1981.

Right: No 08.658 stands over the inspection pits at Landore on 31 December 1981. The bright sunshine entering the depot provides interesting lighting for this study.

Top: This former Class 24 locomotive, No 24.142, survived the cutter's torch when it was converted into a train heating unit and renumbered ADB 968009. Here it is seen standing in Swansea High Street Carriage sidings, on 31 December 1981.

Above: Nos 37.205 and 37.293 stand at the head of a group of locomotives resting from duty at Barry on Sunday 2 August 1981.

Above: Spring 1981 saw the transfer of No 03.382 from the Bristol Bath Road depot to Landore for work on the Burry Port & Gwendraeth Valley line, but before the loco could go into service on the BPGV, it was necessary to lower the cab. Evidence of the welding work which was carried out at Ebbw Junction can be seen here.

Below: A splendid contrast is provided in this photograph of the unique 3,300hp, No 47.901 and the rather less powerful privately-owned locomotive *Planet*, which is normally used at Powell Duffryn Quarries, Machen. This unusual encounter took place at Ebbw Junction MPD on 28 August 1981 when *Planet* had received attention from BR for gearbox and final drive defects. *Bob Masterman*

Above left: Even wet and dull days can provide possibilities for the keen railway photographer. The depressing weather on 25 May 1981 is clearly apparent in this study of No 37.282 at Ebbw Junction, Newport. *Keith Hayward*

Above right: No 03.144 undergoes repairs at Landore on 31 December 1981. The collieries throughout South Wales were closed for the week between Christmas and the New Year, leaving the Class 03 locomotives free for maintenance work.

Below: Nos 37.175 and 47.078 *Sir Daniel Gooch* receive attention at Cardiff's Canton depot on 26 August 1980. From the photograph it can be seen that the Class 47 locomotive has had its wheel bogies removed.

Right: No 47.029 has its wheels turned on the tyre re-profiling machine which is situated in the carriage shed at Canton depot. The photograph was taken on 26 August 1980.

Lightweight vehicles

Below: The first visit of the Class 140 lightweight DMU to the South Wales area took place on 28-30 June 1981, and formed part of its nationwide demonstration tour. During a run from Cardiff to Abercynon on 29 June 1981 the unit is seen here passing the signal gantry at Radyr station; a sight familiar to South Wales enthusiasts.

Bottom: The demonstration tour included two full days in South Wales. On 30 June 1981 the Class 140 ventured to Cynghordy on the Central Wales line and was subjected to gradients in excess of 1:60. The unit performed admirably and is seen here departing from Cynghordy station, bound for Llanelli and Carmarthen.

Above: During January 1982 the Class 140 units began a brief period in revenue earning service on the Central Wales line, but because of gearbox and track circuit problems was withdrawn after a few weeks of operation. Repairs and modifications saw its reintroduction on the Central Wales line in June 1982. In this photograph No 140.001 is passing Ffairfach station and signalbox on the return leg of its first trip in revenue earning service, which was from Swansea to Shrewsbury and back on 4 January 1982. The distant signal, right, is the up fixed distant for Llandeilo.

Below: A unique meeting of the Class 140 and other units occurred on 5 February 1982 after No 140.001 had transported a group of local MPs to Cardiff Queen Street station. The Class 140 was temporarily relieved of duties on the Central Wales line whilst the R3 railbus had a few hours free from duties in the Bristol area to allow MPs to see both vehicles. DMU No C304 looks on and provides an interesting contrast of styles. *June McGregor*

Port Talbot-Llanwern Iron Ore train

Top: The massive Llanwern steelworks provide a typical industrial backdrop for No 56.041 and 56.035 as they lead a train of iron ore empties towards East Usk Junction, Newport en route to Port Talbot on 11 September 1981. Up to five return workings a day are diagrammed to run the 46 miles between Port Talbot and Llanwern. *Bob Masterman*

Above: The 17.10 Cardiff-Crewe service with its five coaches was dwarfed by the massive 30-wagon Port Talbot-Llanwern ore train as the two sped towards Newport on the bright sunny evening of 29 July 1981. No 56.037 *Richard Trevithick* and 56.035 head the ore train.

— Britain's heaviest freight

Above: Nos 56.038 *Western Mail* and 56.037 *Richard Trevithick* are seen at Fairwater, Cardiff on the first occasion that two named Class 56 locomotives were coupled together. This had been specially arranged for a party of VIPs travelling with the Port Talbot-Llanwern ore train on 5 August 1981. *Keith Hayward*

Below: Seen on 14 April 1982 are Nos 56.038 *Western Mail* and 56.035 *Taff Merthyr* as they speed along the up relief line with a load of iron ore for Llanwern Steel Works; Cardiff Pengam Freightliner depot can be seen in the background. *Bob Masterman*

Top: Whilst three Class 37 or two Class 56 locomotives are required to haul the loaded 30 wagon train of ore, two Class 37 locomotives are sufficient to return the empties to Port Talbot. From time to time shortages of Class 56 locomotives make it necessary to use Class 37 traction for the haulage of the ore train. Here Nos 37.300 and 37.177, with a train of empties are seen on 22 March 1982 passing the site of the former Llanharan station, which is between Llantrisant and Bridgend.

Above: Another occasion when a shortage of Class 56 traction had necessitated the use of Class 37 locomotives provides us with a taste of how things used to be; No 37.305, 37.280 and 37.303 leads a loaded train of iron ore to Llanwern, past Steelfab Ltd east of Cardiff on 18 August 1980.

Right: No 56.037 *Richard Trevithick* and 56.044 head the Port Talbot-Llanwern ore train past Rumney, Cardiff on a very hazy morning on 26 March 1982.

Cardiff to Crewe services

Above: Except for Sundays and up until the introduction of the 1981 passenger timetable, services between Cardiff and Crewe were dominated by Class 25 traction. No 25.042 used to be a regular performer on these services and here it is seen crossing the River Usk at Newport on 16 April with the 15.10 ex-Cardiff train.

Left: Pontypool Road was once a busy railway centre, but nowadays the station known simply as Pontypool consists of a wide almost barren expanse of platform which, fortunately for the would-be passengers, was bathed in sunshine on 4 September 1981 when No 33.005 arrived with the 11.50 Cardiff-Crewe service.
Bob Masterman

Top: Adverse weather conditions in South Wales during January 1982 led to a severe disruption of the timetable. No 33.021 accelerates from Cardiff with the 40 minutes late departure of the 15.10 Cardiff-Crewe train on 11 January. Note the two leading PO vehicles which are, under normal circumstances, conveyed on the 20.00 Cardiff-Crewe and 01.47 return services. The low winter sun and reflections from the snow provides a superb illumination of this train.

Above: No 25.224 is seen on its approach to Abergavenny with a six-coach Crewe-Cardiff train on 2 May 1981. *Bob Masterman*

Above: Again No 25.224 is seen in action, here it heads the 12.27 Crewe to Cardiff at Gaer Junction, Newport on 30 September 1980. In the background, No 56.046 awaits entry into Newport Docks with a train of mgr empties from Didcot. *John Chalcraft*

Left: No 47.538 leads the 11.50 Cardiff-Crewe train north of Abergavenny on a typically cold winters day on 23 January 1982.

Bottom left: Class 33 traction was introduced on Cardiff-Crewe services at the same time as the 1981-2 timetable and has since proved to be both popular and successful on this route. On 1 August 1981, No 33.004 was in charge of the 10.00 Crewe-Cardiff service which is seen at Panteg, south of Pontypool. The up and down recess loops at this point are recent, replacing facilities which were displaced when the New Inn by-pass, which opened in 1982, was built on the former railway formation at Pontypool Road. The siding, right, leads to the premises of Fibreglass Ltd.

Coal traffic

Above: Pantyffynnon is a busy focal point for coal from Bettws Drift, Gwaun-Cae-Gerwen opencast site and Abernant colliery as well as washed coal from the Wernos Washery. Two pilots are on duty on most working days and 30 June 1981 was no exception. No 08.354, left, and No 08.659 go about their tasks on a dull summers day.

Below: The Pantyffynnon pilot No 08.658 leads a train of coal from the very productive Bettws drift mine on 4 January 1981. Pilots work the coal along the short branch from Bettws to Pantyffynnon where traffic is either shunted into the nearby Wernos washery, or taken by Class 37s to the more distant washeries at Abernant or Cynheidre.

Below: The old station nameboard remains almost intact on the disused former down platform at Pantyffynnon station, where No 08.659 brings a train of coal from the Wernos Washery on 30 June 1981.

Bottom: Diabolical weather prevailed as this train of loaded coal arrived at Abernant on 4 January 1982. The gradient up to Abernant is very steep and a banker is required to help the loaded train. Here No 37.220 had headed the train whilst No 37.289, left of picture had acted as banker.

Above: No 37.282 leads a train of coal along the South Wales main line near Newport on a bright and sunny 22 June 1981.

Left: No 45.043 *The King's Own Royal Border Regiment* runs close to the M4 motorway as it heads west past Baglan, near Port Talbot, with a train of coal empties on 24 March 1982. It is unusual to see Class 45 traction at the head of a South Wales coal train, this traffic being normally dominated by the Class 37 locomotives.

Above right: No 37.128 passes St Fagans crossing west of Cardiff with a down train of coal empties on a bitterly cold day on 11 December 1981.

Right: A short train of coal empties is in the charge of No 08.799 as it slowly enters Briton Ferry Yard on 25 March 1982.

Top: No 37.269 with a coal freight from Oakdale Colliery slows down as it passes the crossing at Lime Kiln Junction, where the token is returned to the signalman on 11 September 1981.

Above: No 37.230 leads a train of coal from Abertillery New Mine, down the Western Valley just south of Aberbeeg on 11 September 1981. The two Western Valley routes, from Waunllwyd (Ebbw Vale) and Abertillery New Mine, still known to railwaymen as 'Rose Heyworth' colliery, join at Aberbeeg.

Above: No 37.308 slowly pulls away from the NSF Phurnacite Plant at Abercwmboi in the Cynon Valley, south of Aberdare. The train which is seen on 24 March 1982 is en route for Radyr Yard.
Bob Masterman

Below: No 37.289 departs from Maerdy with a train of coal bound for the Phurnacite Plant at Abercwmboi on 13 April 1982. Abercwmboi is in an adjacent valley and is only three and a half miles from Maerdy 'as the crow flies', but the train has to run to Pontypridd, where the locomotive must run round before the next leg of the journey up the Taff and Cynon Valleys to Abercwmboi can be undertaken. A total distance of over 18 miles is covered on this trip.

Right: Heading for the Abercwmboi Phurnacite Plant, and seen between Pontypridd and Abercynon is No 37.284 with a train of coal on 16 November 1981. *Keith Hayward*

Below: Bound for the coke plant at Nantgarw is No 37.162, which is seen departing from Radyr yard on 29 July 1981. Radyr Yard is the focal point for coal traffic movements to and from the valleys inland from Cardiff.

Bottom: Having arrived at Nantgarw Coke Ovens with a train of empties on 21 April 1982, No 37.239 prepares to pick up loaded wagons of coke for Barry Docks from where the coke is exported to Roumania.

Above: No 37.204 slowly pulls its train through the discharge point at Nelson Bog on 23 February 1982 where mining waste from the nearby Taff Merthyr and Deep Navigation collieries is tipped. The line nearest the camera is the route from these and other collieries to the Rhymney Valley at Ystrad Mynach. *Bob Masterman*

Below: Crossing the road at Newport Docks is No 08.780 as it propels a train of coal empties alongside the Main Basin on 22 January 1982. The export of South Wales coal through this port resumed in 1980. *Keith Hayward*

Left: No 37.257 departs with a train of coal from Cwm Colliery on 22 March 1982 and heads towards the main line at Llantrisant.

Below: Llantrisant is the point on the main line where the branches from Cwm and Coed Ely collieries and coke ovens join the main line. No 37.241 passes the former Llantrisant goods shed and snakes across to the up main line with a train of loaded coke wagons and empties on 22 March 1982. *John Chalcraft*

Right: A mishap occurred at Llantrisant on 23 June 1982 when a train of empties and loaded coal wagons led by No 37.138 from Severn Tunnel Junction became derailed as it crossed from the down main line into Llantrisant Yard. The blocking of the up and down main lines for several hours led to passenger and freight services being diverted from the main line to the Vale of Glamorgan line. *Bob Ranson*

Above left: The driver of No 37.240 with a train of empties bound for Cwm Colliery receives the token from the signalman at Cowbridge Road crossing near Llantrisant on 17 June 1982. *Bob Ranson*

Left: Passing the remains of Llynfi Power Station is No 37.218 heading towards Tondu with a train of coal from Maesteg on 25 March 1982.

Above: No 37.229 arrives at Nantymoel at the top end of the Ogmore Valley with a train of empty coal wagons for Wyndham Colliery on a wet overcast day on 11 March 1982. When loaded, the train will take the coal to the Ogmore Valley Central Washery, three miles down the valley.

Right: Coal from the collieries at Blaengarw and Maesteg is taken via Tondu to the Ogmore Vale Washery for washing. Here No 37.229 passes the Ogmore Vale Washery with a train of coal from Maesteg on 11 March 1982.

Above: No 37.230 passes Caedu signalbox on 17 February 1982 on the Ogmore Vale branch with a train of coal for the washery. The track layout is such that the train must pull up past the signalbox before reversing back into the washery which is to the left in the photograph. *Bob Masterman*

Below: No 37.181 heads a train of coal empties towards Blaengarw on 18 May 1982, where it picks up a load of coal for the Ogmore Vale Washery.

Top: Only one trip a day goes to Aberpergwm in the Neath Valley, and that is usually early in the morning. Here the crew of No 37.293, which brought the Swansea Docks-Aberpergwm train, take a tea break at the colliery before returning south with a load of coal on 18 June 1982. *Michael Rhodes*

Above: A short coal freight led by No 47.082 and bound for the coal merchant's yard at Milford Haven is seen travelling across country between Haverfordwest and Johnston on 8 April 1982. As British Rail continue to strive for economies and greater efficiency such trains clearly have a very limited future.

Central Wales line

Top left: Two splendid viaducts are a feature of the Welsh section of the Central Wales line. The southernmost of these is the curving 18 arch Cynghordy viaduct which has a span of 36ft 6in between arches and carries the Central Wales line 93ft above the valley floor. The viaduct is 'listed' as a structure of special architectural and historic interest. Here No C621, with headlight switched on, forms the 14.58 Swansea-Shrewsbury service on 30 June 1981.

Left: The 10.46 Shrewsbury-Swansea service crosses the architecturally stylish Knucklas viaduct, with its castellated end-turrets on 8 May 1982. The train is receding from the camera and is only three miles into Wales, having crossed the border at Knighton.

Above: Railmen look on as the driver of the 12.25 Swansea-Shrewsbury train receives the token from the signalman before proceeding into Pantyffynnon station on 30 June 1981. As far as Pantyffynnon the train has been under the control of Port Talbot panel box and the token applies for the section on to Llandeilo.

Right: No C620 forms the 15.43 Shrewsbury-Swansea service which is seen near Ammanford on 8 May 1982.

No C615 traverses the unmanned Berthddu crossing just north of Sugar Loaf Tunnel with the 15.48 Swansea-Shrewsbury service on 8 May 1982.

Freightliner and Speedlink trains

Above: Now a scene from the past on the main line near St Fagans; No 45.037 leads an up Freightliner train on 28 August 1980 under the viaduct which used to carry the old Barry Railway main line. This viaduct was demolished on 17 October 1981 to make way for a proposed road linking Barry to the M4 motorway.

Above: No 56.040 *Oystermouth* is seen here shortly before departing with the 16.10 Freightliner train from Danygraig Freightliner terminal in Swansea. The locomotive had been named at Swansea High Street station earlier on in the day on 25 March 1982.

Below: No 37.302 brings an up block train of Speedlink wagons past Undy, on the approach to Severn Tunnel Junction on 5 November 1981. *Bob Masterman*

Below: Marshalling its train at Cardiff's Pengam Freightliner terminal is No 47.193 on 13 October 1981.

Bottom: No 46.056 leads an up Freightliner train past Alexandra Dock Junction Yard, Newport on 15 April 1981. The line in the immediate foreground which crosses over the main line, used to link Park Junction, on the Western Valley line, to Courtybella Junction, on the lines to Newport's docks area. This line has been taken out of use since this photograph was taken.

Above: No 45.050 approaches Llantrisant with a Speedlink service from Severn Tunnel Junction to Margam on 29 October 1981. *Bob Masterman*

Right: No split-headcode Class 37 locomotives are based in the South Wales area though occasionally they do make an appearance. Here No 37.067 leads an up Speedlink service over Bishton flyover on 24 March 1982. The flyover was built in the early 1960s to take the up relief line from the seaward side of the main line in the west (for the Llanwern and Newport Docks) to the landward side of the main line in the east (for the up yards at Severn Tunnel Junction). *Bob Masterman*

Below: The inaugural Speedlink service, in the charge of No 37.267, leaves the Ford engine plant at Bridgend shortly after the official opening of the new Ford branch line on 15 January 1980. Note the Continental train ferry wagons at the rear. *Tom Clift*

South Wales to the Midlands and the North

An impression of power is created in this photograph of a Class 47 leading the rapidly accelerating 11.45 Cardiff-Newcastle train on 10 June 1981. The train is seen passing Roath Goods yard in Cardiff.

Caerdydd Canolog
Cardiff Central

BIRMINGHAM

Left: No 45.130 in ex-works condition nears Newport with the 17.44 Cardiff-Sheffield service on 29 July 1981. Air conditioned stock which was introduced on to this route in the late 1970s is being replaced by HSTs in 1982, and the air-conditioned locomotive-hauled vehicles will then be transferred to services between South Wales and Manchester.

Centre left: Dense freezing fog at Cardiff Central station greets the arrival of the 06.02 Sheffield-Cardiff on 15 January 1982. The locomotive and stock later formed the 11.45 return working from Cardiff to Newcastle.

Bottom left: A summer through train working which was dropped from the 1982-3 timetable was the 13.10 (SO) Barry Island-Birmingham service. London Midland Region DMU sets were used on this train which is seen passing through Magor between Newport and Severn Tunnel Junction on 1 August 1981.

Right: As the 10.42 Swansea-Paddington train dives into Hillfield Tunnel, Newport, an unidentified Class 45 emerges with the 08.25 Manchester Piccadilly-Cardiff service on 11 September 1981. Note the signalling and staff warning boards for reversible working.

Below: The first cross-country HST service from South Wales ran on 17 May 1982 when the 1982-3 passenger timetable was introduced. Here on its inaugural service the 06.52 Swansea-Newcastle train is seen passing near Canton depot on its approach to Cardiff. The 15.38 service to Birmingham is also formed by an HST and from October 1982 the 10.00 Cardiff-Newcastle and the 17.37 Cardiff-Leeds were replaced by HST services.

Naming ceremonies

Above: Mrs Cherry Michell, great great great granddaughter of Richard Trevithick revealed the name of her famous forebear on the side of No 56.037 *Richard Trevithick* in a ceremony at Merthyr Tydfil on 23 July 1981.

Left: Sir Derek Ezra, Chairman of the National Coal Board, with his back to the camera, is clapped by Sir Peter Parker, Chairman of British Rail, as he officially names No 56.035, *Taff Merthyr*, after the colliery where the ceremony took place on 9 November 1981. The choice of name was seen as a tribute to the close links that exist between the two nationalised industries in South Wales.
Keith Hayward

Right: The alternative side to naming ceremonies is portrayed here. As the Mayor of Swansea performs the official naming of *Oystermouth* the plate on the other side of loco No 56.040 is discreetly revealed by a railwayman at Swansea High Street station on 25 March 1982. The naming was to mark the 175th Anniversary of the Oystermouth Railway — the world's first passenger carrying railway.

Oyste

Steel traffic

Above: Steel coil for Ebbw Vale and a special sticker for No 37.185 commemorates the official opening of a new single tracked line at Rogerstone. The realignment of the track was made necessary by the road improvement plans of Gwent County Council. The former double tracked section, on the right, was removed a few days after this photograph was taken on 24 November 1981.

Below: No 46.048 leads a train of steel rails through Magor on 25 July 1980. The train which is seen on the up main line, transferred to the up relief line moments later. *Bob Masterman*

Top: A train of empty steel carriers in the charge of No 37.210 leaves Alexandra Dock Junction Yard, Newport on 15 April 1981. The lines to the left lead to Newport Docks.

Above: Unusual traction for the Western Valleys is No 31.424 as it leads a train of steel coil empties from Ebbw Vale, on to the main line at Gaer Junction, Newport on 11 September 1981. Two months later the route on which the train is seen was reduced to single track.

Right: No 47.240 with a down train of steel coil from Margam passes the massive Llandarcy oil refinery on the Swansea District line on 25 March 1982. The line leaving the picture to the right is the rail access to the refinery. The steel coil is bound for the Trostre Tinplate Works at Llanelli.

Below: No 47.230 with a train of continuously-welded rails from the Hookagate rail welding depot near Shrewsbury passes through the countryside near St Fagans, Cardiff on 28 August 1980.

Royal trains

Above: During the early 1980s No 47.511 *Thames* seemed to be the favoured locomotive for the haulage of Royal trains in South Wales and indeed on the three Royal visits featured in this section this locomotive was always seen in charge. Here No 47.511 *Thames* with its special headlight, travels along the Central Wales line north of Pantyffynon during the visit of the Prince and Princess of Wales on 29 October 1981. This was the Royal Couple's first visit to the Principality following their marriage in July. The ban on main line locomotive-haulage on the Central Wales line was temporarily lifted for this tour but the speed of the train was restricted to 30mph.

Below: The Royal Party disembarked at Builth Road, and continued the next stage of their tour by road. From Builth Road the train continued to Llandrindod Wells where the locomotive ran round before returning south. Here the train of 'empty stock' which included some very large and conspicuous members of the Security Forces, is seen crossing the River Tywi at Llandeilo.

Above: By the time the empty stock had reached the South Wales main line the bright sunny weather of the early morning had turned to rain. Here No 47.511 *Thames* with its headlight now removed, heads through the pouring rain at Miskin.

Below: On Maundy Thursday 8 April 82 HM Queen visited St Davids Cathedral in West Wales where she presented Maundy Money to Senior Citizens. The Royal train which conveyed the Royal Party to Fishguard Harbour had spent the previous evening stabled on the Ministry of Defence branch at Trecwn, and is seen here shortly after joining the main Fishguard branch at Letterston Junction.
Phil Taylor

Top: HM Queen and the Duke of Edinburgh disembarked from their train at Fishguard Harbour from where the empty stock was returned east. Here locomotive and stock is seen passing Wolf's Castle.

Above: On 30 April 1982 HRH Prince of Wales had an afternoon engagement in Carmarthen followed by an evening engagement in Cardiff. Here the five-carriage Royal Train which is seen approaching Miskin Loops on the main line, takes the Prince of Wales to his Cardiff engagement.

Burry Port & Gwendraeth Valley

Above: The guard closes the crossing gates to road traffic at Pontyberem and waits for Nos 03.142 and 03.145 to lead the 13.10-booked Burry Port-Cwmmawr train of coal empties on 5 March 1981. Three Class 03 locomotives were involved in the hauling of this train, the photograph fails to show No 03.120 which was providing added propulsion at the rear of the train.

Left: An example of low clearances occurs at the point where the BPGV line passes under the main Swansea to Carmarthen line near Burry Port. Here No 03.145, 03.151, 03.152 are close to this point as they lead a train of washed coal from the Coedbach Washery to Burry Port on 10 July 1981. The proposed new link between Codebach and Kidwelly will enable modern wagons, hauled by Class 37 locomotives, to operate traffic from the washery.
Bob Masterman

Top right: Nos 03.151 and 03.120 lead a train of empties north past Pinged on a Saturday working on a dull, damp 23 January 1982.
Bob Masterman

Right: At the head of the BPGV line at Cwmmawr, Nos 03.145, 03.142 and 03.120 organise their train before moving south to the Coedbach Washery on 5 March 1981.

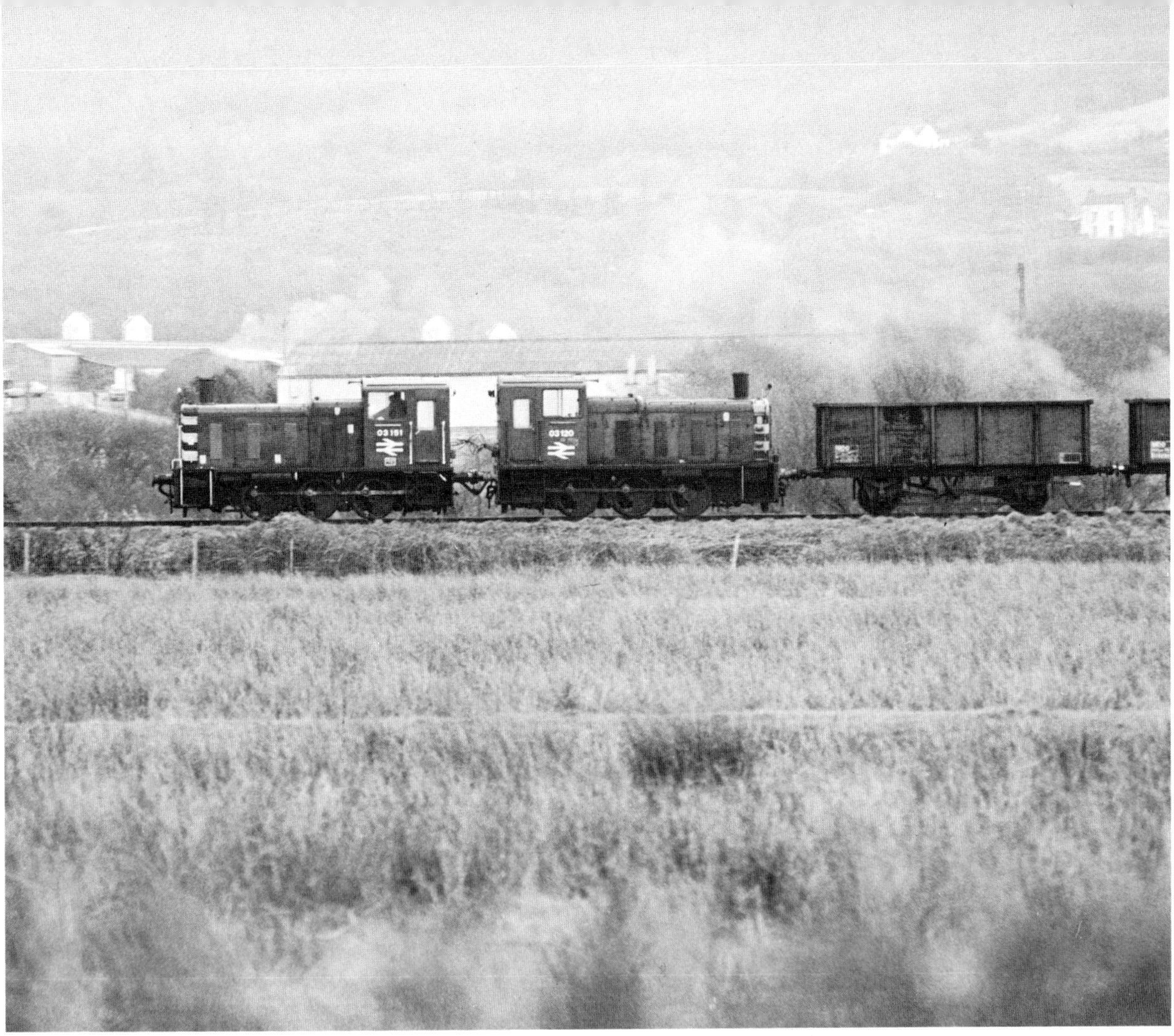
03 151
03 120

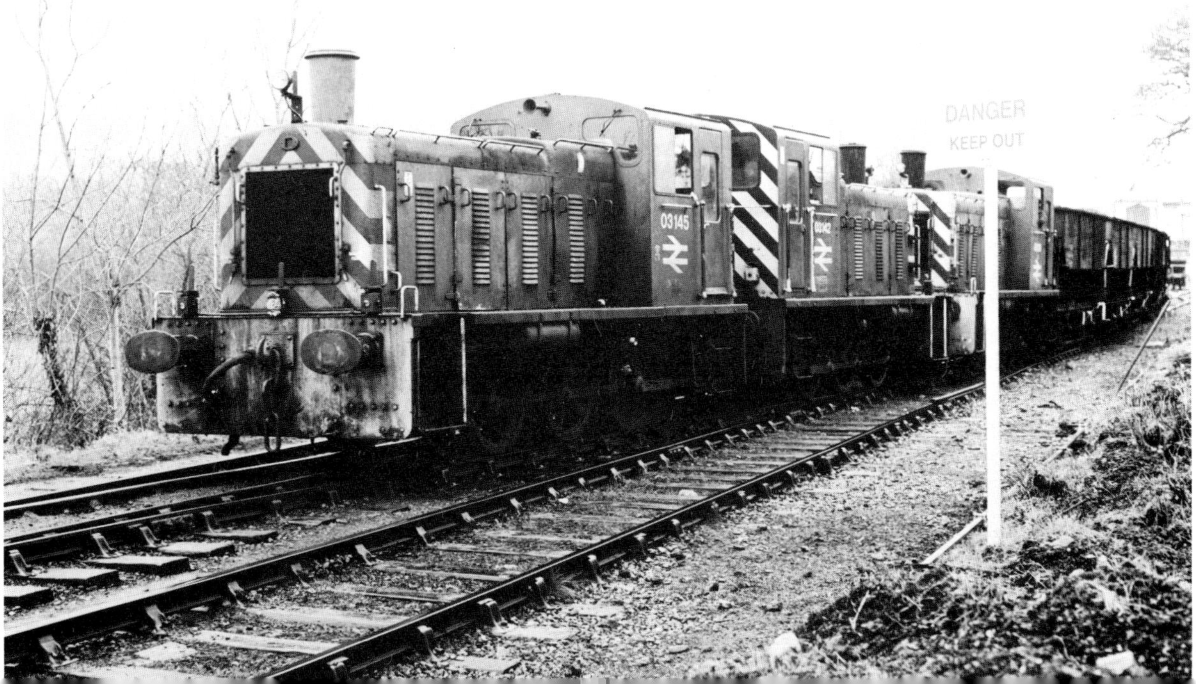
03145
DANGER
KEEP OUT

Excursions and Special trains

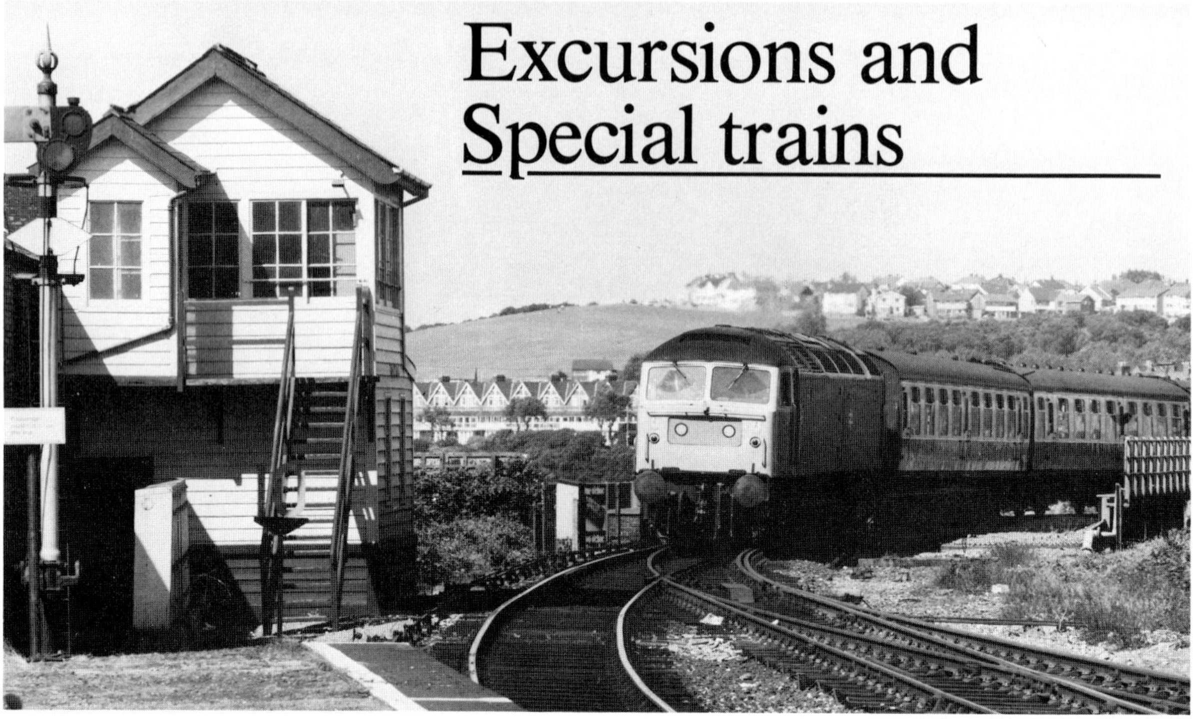

Above left: Barry Island is a popular venue for the day tripper and this is reflected in the number of ADEX specials that visit the resort on summer weekends. Here No 47.121 leads a packed train from Paddington on 2 August 1981.

Left: No 47.096 heads a mystery excursion from Treherbert on 2 August 1981 and provides the opportunity of seeing a loco-hauled passenger train in the Rhondda Valley. The train is seen just south of Porth station.

Top: Interesting traction is provided by No 46.036 for the homeward-bound Merrymaker special from Barry Island to Alfreton. The train is seen approaching Cogan station on 26 July 1981.

Above right: To mark the impending retirement of Sir Derek Ezra from his post as Chairman of the National Coal Board, Sir Derek visited several collieries in South Wales on 10 May 1982. Here the special train consisting of No 31.413 and an Observation Saloon is seen departing from Oakdale Colliery from where it went on to Celenyn South Colliery via Lime Kiln Junction.

Bottom right: HH Pope John Paul II visited Cardiff on 2 June 1982 and a large number of special trains were arranged to bring people to Cardiff. Here Nos 31.139 and 31.216 lead a return special to Portsmouth along the South Wales main line.

Above: No album on South Wales would be complete without featuring a rugby special. This special, taking supporters from Carmarthen to the Wales v France international at Cardiff on 6 February 1982, is seen emerging from Lonlas tunnel on the Swansea District line in the charge of No 45.077.

Right: The last working of a locomotive-hauled excursion along the Central Wales line occurred on 21 December 1980 when No 40.030 worked a train from Leeds to Llandrindod Wells; only the second occasion that a Class 40 locomotive had worked along the Central Wales line. A ban was brought in to force on 1 January 1981 to exclude heavy loco-haulage from the Central Wales line. The aim of this was to delay any future track renewal work. *Tom Clift*

Below right: A rare event took place on 5 May 1982 when DMU No B822 travelled along the Ford branch at Bridgend and traversed the level crossing over the A48 before continuing into the Ford Engine Plant. This special charter organised by the Institute of Civil Engineers, was the first passenger train to venture over this level crossing. Photographing normal freight traffic on this branch, which opened in 1980, is difficult because most movements take place in the hours of darkness.

Above: An Easter Sunday mystery excursion from Treherbert is seen here between Pontypridd and Treforest on 11 April 1982. No 47.105 heads the eight-carriage train.

Left: Although South Wales based drivers are not trained to drive Class 50 locomotives, these locomotives do occasionally find their way into the area. One such occasion was on 24 October 1981 when No 50.023 led a 'Rail Ale' special from High Wycombe to Cardiff via Paddington. The train was photographed at Newport in what could only be described as atrocious weather conditions.
John Chalcraft

Above: Three two-car DMUs form an Easter Saturday Rambler's Excursion from Blackpool to Llandrindod Wells on 10 April 1982. It called by request at halts between Knighton and Llandrindod Wells and set down ramblers who walked during the day and were picked up at stations along the line during the return trip. This was the first excursion from the north end of the line since the ban on locomotive-hauled excursions. The train which was made up of London Midland Region DMUs carried a portable spotlight which had been converted from an oil tail lamp. *Tom Clift*

Right: A two-car DMU from Liverpool was sufficient to carry Everton football supporters to their club's away match with Swansea City on 1 May 1982. Here the train is seen scurrying through the countryside near Miskin. The success of Swansea City Football Club and their promotion to Division One of the Football League at the end of the 1980-1 season has seen an increase in the number of specials both to and from the city during the football season.

Parcels trains

Above: No 37.183 departs from Milford Haven with the afternoon parcels train to Paddington on 28 May 1981. This service finished a month later as a consequence of the withdrawal of British Rail's collect and deliver service.

Left: Snow carpets the ground as No 47.421 heads a Paddington-bound parcels train out of Cardiff on 11 January 1982.

Above: No 47.112 leads the 18.20 Swansea-Paddington Premium parcels service past St Georges on 20 August 1981. The low sun angle and the backlighting provides a pleasing illumination for this train.

Right: The 12.28 Swansea-Paddington Premium parcels train led by No 37.187 is seen passing through the countryside at St Georges on 20 June 1981.

Chemical and Oil trains

Above: Vynyl Chloride Monomer trains which run between BP Chemicals Baglan Bay and BP Chemicals Barry are usually in the hands of Class 37 or Class 47 traction; on this occasion however No 31.117, which is normally based at Old Oak Common, headed the train of westbound empty tanks past Llantrisant on 7 June 1982. At the time of writing BP Chemicals announced that the supply of chemical feedstock from their Baglan Bay plant to that of Barry would cease shortly, with the result that this particular train movement has an uncertain future.

Left: No 47.242 leads a train of empty tanks, including those for propane and butane, towards Maindee West Junction, Newport on 16 April 1981. The train which had travelled down the North and West line through Hereford is en route for one of the oil refineries at Milford Haven.

Left: No 46.033 leads an Avonmouth to Swansea train of sulphuric acid tanks along the South Wales down relief east of Cardiff on 1 June 1982.

Bottom left: No 37.177 heads a down train of oil empties through the snow at St Georges on 11 December 1981.

Right: On a dull and misty morning No 08.351 arrives at Radyr Yard with a train of tanks from Penarth North Curve on 8 February 1982. These tanks had just been used to supply locomotive diesel fuel to Canton MPD. *Bob Masterman*

Below: Class 56 traction is fairly unusual for an oil train. Here No 56.035 *Taff Merthyr* approaches Miskin loops on 28 May 1982.

Above: No 47.098 leads a train of 100-ton oil tankers from Milford Haven on 9 April 1982. The train is seen at Llanfallteg West between Clunderwen and Whitland, in West Wales.

Right: A Class 47 locomotive leads a train of 100-ton oil tankers through St Fagans to the Gulf Oil Refinery at Milford Haven on the 16 October 1981. Temporary speed restrictions were in force whilst demolition experts packed high explosives into the structure of the former Barry Railway viaduct, in readiness for its demolition in the early hours of the following day. The demolition resulted in the main South Wales line being closed for a mere 24 hours in which time a length of track was lifted, the viaduct was blown up and removed and the track then relayed.

Below right: No 47.079 *G. J. Churchward* leads a chemicals train from Baglan Bay along the main line between Llanharan and Llantrisant on 22 March 1982.

Passenger services to Severnside and the South

Class 118 three-car suburban set No B460 awaits departure from Chepstow with the 11.32 Gloucester to Newport service on 6 May 1981. *Bob Masterman*

Top: No 45.125 leads the 18.10 Cardiff-Portsmouth Harbour service along the main line east of Cardiff on 10 April 1982.

Above: The first regular use of Class 33 traction on South Wales passenger services started in January 1981 when they began to appear on the 15.30 Bristol Temple Meads-Cardiff service. On 9 January 1981 during their first week of operation, No 33.004 is seen at platform 2 at Cardiff Central station waiting to depart with the return 17.20 Cardiff-Bristol Temple Meads working. Although Class 33s are now a common sight in South Wales, and operate services through to Milford Haven, Fishguard and Crewe, at the time of writing no Class 33s had been transferred to South Wales depots. Diagrams are arranged so that maintenance work can still be carried out at Eastleigh.

Right: Here the 15.30 Bristol Temple Meads-Cardiff train is seen on 15 April 1981 passing Gaer Junction, Newport.

Above: More Class 33 action in the shape of No 33.035 as it leads the 12.10 Portsmouth Harbour-Cardiff train along the South Wales main line just west of Newport on 10 April 1982.

Left: No 45.111 *Grenadier Guardsman* is seen on 24 December 1981 with the 12.10 Cardiff-Portsmouth Harbour train full of passengers heading home for the Christmas holiday.

Other freight

Above: Empty Presflo cement wagons led by No 47.420 arrive at Aberthaw on 21 July 1981 near the end of their journey to the nearby Cement works. The tracks to the right lead down to Aberthaw Power Station.

Left: No 47.241 leads an Aberthaw to Carmarthen cement train out of Porthkerry number one tunnel, near Barry, on 30 January 1982. *Keith Hayward*

Top right: The former Pontypool Road-Monmouth branch now terminates at Glascoed where the Ministry of Defence have an Ordinance Factory. Here No 37.277 with a train of Government supplies heads along the Glascoed branch towards Little Mill Junction on 23 February 1981. *John Vaughan*

Right: To mark the naming of No 56.037 *Richard Trevithick* at Merthyr Tydfil the replica of Trevithick's Penydarren locomotive was transported to Merthyr Tydfil station. The replica locomotive which was built by the Welsh Industrial & Maritime Museum, Cardiff, was transported by road to Roath Coal sidings where it was loaded on to a low level transporter. Here on 22 July 1981, the day before the ceremony, No 08.787 propels the Penydarren locomotive out of the coal sidings before conveying it it to Cardiff Central station where it was stabled overnight in readiness for its journey to Merthyr Tydfil.

Above: No 37.190 leads a Llandeilo Junction-bound mixed freight from Trecwn and Fishguard Harbour, along the Fishguard Harbour branch through Wolf's Castle on 3 September 1981. The train is made up of wagons of Government supplies from the Ministry of Defence Establishment at Trecwn, as well as domestic coal and bunker oil empties from Fishguard Harbour.

Right: A low midwinter sun illuminates No 45.042 and its train of loose-coupled railfreight and coal wagons, as they head for Severn Tunnel Junction in January 1980. The train is seen on the up relief near Llanwern. *John Vaughan*

Below right: What could easily be mistaken as a rail guards outing is seen, in the charge of No 37.217, as it arrives at Severn Tunnel Junction on 5 November 1981. On the right No 37.183 stands at the stop block after having brought in a freight transfer from the downside yards. *Bob Masterman*

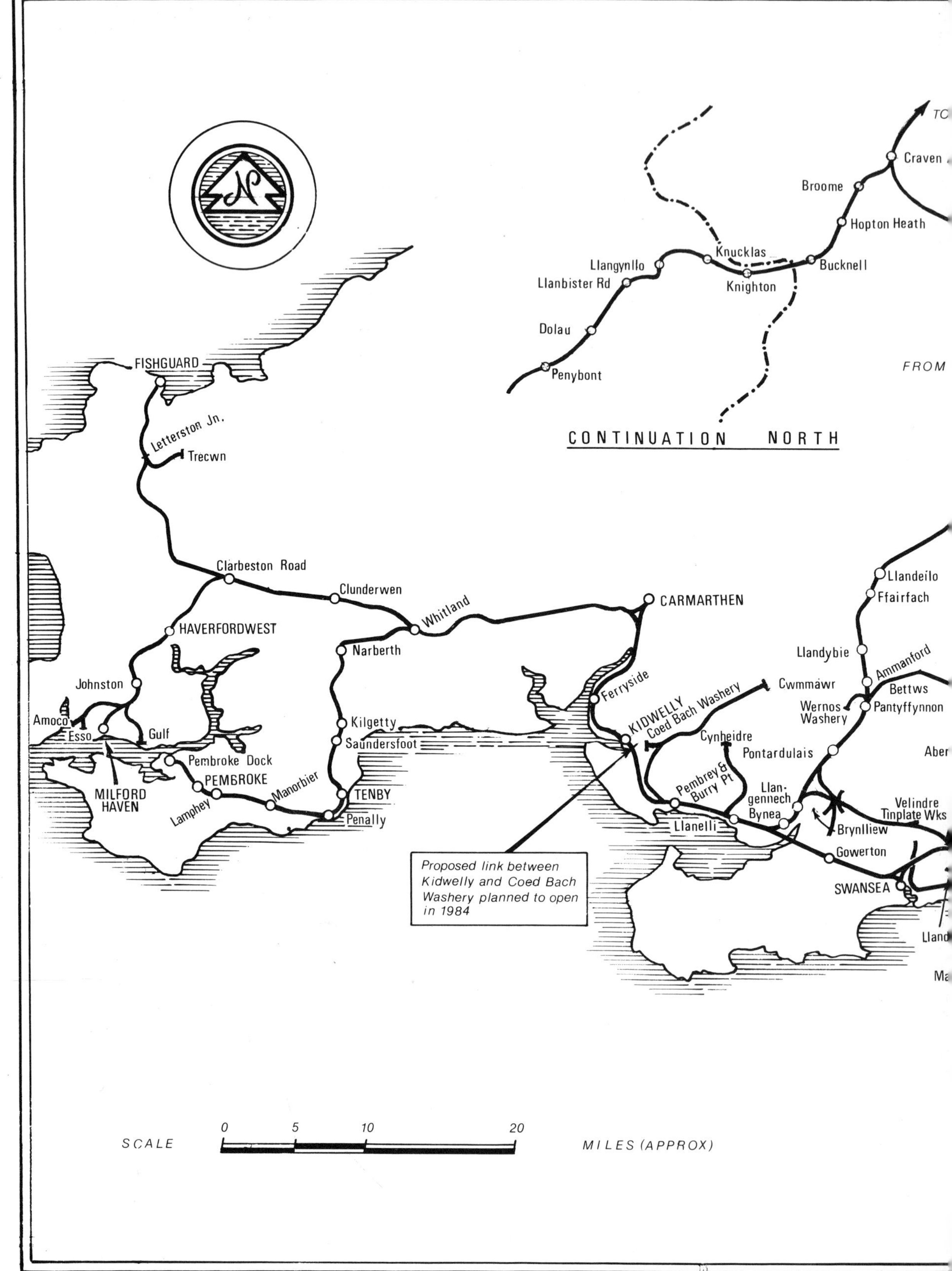
FISHGUARD
Letterston Jn.
Trecwn
Clarbeston Road
Clunderwen
Whitland
CARMARTHEN
HAVERFORDWEST
Narberth
Johnston
Amoco
Esso
Gulf
MILFORD HAVEN
Pembroke Dock
PEMBROKE
Lamphey
Manorbier
Kilgetty
Saundersfoot
TENBY
Penally
Ferryside
KIDWELLY
Coed Bach Washery
Cwmmawr
Cynheidre
Pembrey & Burry Pt
Llanelli
Pontardulais
Llan-gennech
Bynea
Brynlliew
Velindre Tinplate Wks
Gowerton
SWANSEA
Llandeilo
Ffairfach
Llandybie
Ammanford
Bettws
Wernos Washery
Pantyffynnon
Proposed link between Kidwelly and Coed Bach Washery planned to open in 1984
CONTINUATION NORTH
Penybont
Dolau
Llanbister Rd
Llangynllo
Knucklas
Knighton
Bucknell
Hopton Heath
Broome
Craven
FROM
SCALE
0
5
10
20
MILES (APPROX)